PISCES

This Book Belongs To

_____

D1270267

PISCES

The Sign of the Fish
February 20–March 20

By Teresa Celsi
and Michael Yawney

Ariel Books

Andrews and McMeel
Kansas City

PISCES

Copyright © 1994 by Armand Eisen. All rights
reserved. Printed in Hong Kong. No part of this
book may be used or reproduced in any manner
whatsoever without written permission except in
the case of reprints in the context of reviews. For
information write Andrews and McMeel, a Univer-
sal Press Syndicate Company, 4900 Main Street,
Kansas City, Missouri 64112.

ISBN: 0–8362–3076–0
Library of Congress Catalog Card Number:
93–73370

Contents

The text of this book was set in Bembo
and the display in Caslon Open Face
by Crane Typesetting Service, Inc.,
West Barnstable, Massachusetts.

Book design and illustrations by
JUDITH A. STAGNITTO

Aquarius) are clever and intellectual. Water signs (Cancer, Scorpio, and Pisces) are emotional and empathetic.

Each sign has one of three qualities—*cardinal*, *fixed*, or *mutable*—which shows how it operates. Cardinal signs (Aries, Cancer, Libra, and Capricorn) use their energy to lead in a direct, forceful way. Fixed signs (Taurus, Leo, Scorpio, and Aquarius) harness energy and use it to organize and consolidate. Mutable signs (Gemini, Virgo, Sagittarius, and Pisces) use energy to transform and change.

Every sign has a different combination of an element and a quality. When the positions of all the twelve planets are added to a chart, you can begin to

Astrology

An Introduction

Early in our history, as humankind changed from hunter-gatherers to farmers, they left the forests and moved to the plains, where they could raise plants and livestock. While they guarded their animals at night, the herders gazed up at the sky. They watched the stars circle Earth, counted the days between moons, and perceived an order in the universe.

appreciate the complexity of each individual. Astrology does not simplify people by shoving them into twelve personality boxes; rather, the details of your chart will be amazingly complex, inspiring the same awe those early herders must have felt while gazing up into the mystery of the heavens.

The Sign of the Fish

Pisces, a water sign, is ruled by the planet Neptune, named after the Roman god of the sea. In astrology, water represents the emotions, and the last sign of the zodiac is most at home within the fluid world of feelings.

Like the ocean, which has no borders and is swept by strong currents, the Piscean world is never still. Emotional undercurrents are always moving the Fish. This sign hates monotony and restrictions, preferring a constantly changing environment in which it can continue to evolve. Because it is driven by emotions, Pisces can go through sudden, often bewildering, mood swings.

The symbol of Pisces, two fish swimming in opposite directions yet tied together, hints at the duality of this sign, which is often pulled between the material world and the spiritual world. Learning to live in both worlds simultaneously, by dissolving the boundaries between mind and heart, soul and body, is one of the key lessons this sign must learn.

Character and Personality

As the last sign of the zodiac, Pisces contains some of all the other signs. This sign's mutable nature gives it a chameleonlike ability to take on the qualities of other people. For example, if Pisces dates a sports fan, the Fish is sure to know the score. If Pisces' roommate is a gourmet, the Fish will learn to cook.

One explanation is that Pisces does

not act, it reacts. This sign tends to respond to others rather than to initiate activity. The Fish needs motivation and is inspired by a wide range of people.

Leaving itself open to the influence of others makes Pisces particularly vulnerable to bad situations or manipulative people. To protect itself, the Fish doesn't fight, it evades. It develops the ability to pull out of bad relationships quickly or simply to avoid any potentially disturbing issues.

Because Pisces needs others for stimulation and fulfillment, the Fish can easily become dependent, so it is always wary of getting caught in a net. Anytime it senses a hook, such as marriage or some other binding responsibility, its first reaction is to swim away.

In the watery world of the Fish, there are no boundaries. This sign has a tolerance for ambiguities that would drive other signs crazy. Nothing is clearly black or white or right or wrong to Pisces because it believes all things are relative. Truth is a gray area to the Fish, and it has no qualms about shading the unpleasant ones. Every decision is somehow right, often causing Pisces to be indecisive.

Practical matters usually bore the imaginative Fish, who connects more strongly to the world of dreams and emotions. Pisces has a natural radar that picks up the emotions of those around it, making the Fish amazingly empathetic. When someone else is in pain, Pisces tries to alleviate the distress because it feels the hurt so keenly itself.

Living in the world of emotions can be draining, and all Pisces need some time alone. In the back of its mind, the Fish keeps a fantasy file that it can pull out at will to take a short mental vacation. It is common to see Pisces sitting silently, staring into space with a vague smile, happy in its own world.

Signs and Symbols

Each sign in the zodiac is ruled by a different planet. Pisces is ruled by Neptune, named after the ancient Roman god of the sea. The animal associated with Pisces is the fish, and this sign is symbolized by two fish swimming in opposite directions yet tied together. One fish represents the physical body, the other represents the soul.

The last sign of the zodiac, Pisces

combines the element of water (emotions) with the mutable quality of transforming energy. Receptive, giving, concerned, and sometimes reclusive, those born under this sign are emotionally and spiritually sensitive and concerned with spiritual enlightenment.

Pisces rules the feet and is linked with Thursday. Its lucky number is eleven. Platinum and tin are its metals, aquamarine is its color, and chrysolite is its gemstone.

Plants linked with Pisces are seaweed, moss, and the water lily. Its foods are seafood, cucumbers, pumpkins, and melons.

Health and Fitness

Most Pisces have sensitive constitutions but can be quite healthy if they balance their strong emotions with good diet, proper exercise, fresh air, and sunlight. In fact, outdoor activities are excellent therapy for anything that troubles Pisces.

Since Pisces rules the feet, injuries and ailments such as fallen arches, bunions, and even stubbed toes often afflict this sign. But the Fish responds quickly to such treatments as foot baths, reflexology, and orthotics.

Problems with the liver are also common for Pisces, because of its low tolerance to toxins. Alcohol, drugs, cigarettes, and coffee should be consumed in moderation or eliminated.

Pisces is not always athletic and may have difficulty sticking to the most modest fitness program. However, swimming is a terrific exercise for this sign, which never loses its love of the water. Soothing and invigorating, an aquatic workout is the ideal way for the Fish to keep fit.

Home and Family

Pisces' idea of family usually includes a large group of friends who rely on this sign for a shoulder to cry on. The Pisces' home will be a warm and welcoming place to those who come for tea and sympathy—never mind whether the house is tidy! Homemaking is not an art the Fish cares about cultivating. Though this sign's home is highly original in decor, it is rarely a

Amateur theater attracts Pisces because it likes the opportunity to shed its personality and take on another. Many Fish are avid movie buffs, especially fond of fantasy films and emotion-charged dramas.

This creative water sign loves pictures of all kinds, especially—what else—watercolors! But its greatest enthusiasm is for photography. Every step, from aiming the camera to making the prints, fascinates this sign.

Anything that exercises its creativity pleases Pisces, but probably its favorite pastime of all is just lying on the sofa daydreaming.

Love Among the Signs

What is attraction? What is love? Throughout the centuries, science has tried and failed to come up with a satisfying explanation for the mysterious connection between two people.

For the astrologer, the answer is clear. The position of the planets at the time of your birth creates a pattern that influences you throughout your lifetime.

When your pattern meets another person's, the two of you might clash or harmonize.

Why this mysterious connection occurs can be explored only by completing charts for both individuals. But even if the chemistry is there, will it be a happy relationship? Will it last? No one can tell for certain.

Every relationship requires give-and-take, and an awareness of the sun sign relationships can help with this process. The sun sign influences conscious behavior. Does your lover catalog the items in the medicine cabinet? Chances are you have a Virgo on your hands. Do you like to spend your weekends running while

Pisces with Aries
(March 21–April 20)

T his can be a good match. Both
Pisces and Aries are guided
more by instinct than by intel-
lect. The difference is that Pisces lives
to feel and Aries lives to act. But Pisces
finds the Ram's decisiveness alluring and
will benefit from its energy. In turn, the
Ram will get all the flattery and sympathy it craves from the Fish.

Aries always wants its way and is at-

tracted to Pisces' willingness to let it take charge. The Ram is also drawn to Pisces' extraordinary sensitivity to its moods and needs. Though Aries may act like a loner, it actually hides a secret need to be nurtured, which Pisces instinctively senses.

In lovemaking, this is a steamy combination, with passionate, emotional Aries sweeping tender Pisces off its feet. However, Pisces' delicate emotions require sensitive handling, or the Fish will swim away. For this affair to stay hot, Aries must cultivate some diplomacy—not an easy task for the rambunctious Ram. Though self-centered and domineering at times, Aries loves

with a simple intensity, and Pisces will enjoy the Ram's romantic idealism.

On the negative side, Aries' aggressive nature may alarm Pisces, who avoids confrontation whenever possible. When Pisces attempts to evade an issue, it only fuels Aries' anger—and quick temper. However, the Ram forgives and forgets easily. If Pisces can learn to do the same and let go of old grievances, prolonged conflicts can be avoided and harmony restored.

Aries should not make the mistake of thinking that Pisces' desire to avoid conflict means the Fish is a wimp. In the short run, Aries may win arguments, but over time Pisces always gets what it

wants and, as a water sign, could extinguish Aries' fire if it chose to do so.

Money is a challenge for this couple: They never seem to have it. Aries will probably be a little better off than Pisces, but since neither is apt to save for a rainy day, it might be wise for these two to seek out the services of a professional money manager.

If the gentle Fish can learn to live with the Ram's zealous behavior and the Ram can slow its madcap pace enough to allow time for togetherness, this could be a dynamic, lasting relationship.

Pisces with Taurus
(April 21–May 21)

When these two first meet, down-to-earth Taurus may seem to have little in common with a dreamer like Pisces. Taurus is a slow-moving earth sign firmly planted in the physical world. The Bull believes in all that can be experienced through the five senses; the Fish is involved with invisible silent worlds,

where depth of feeling and spirituality are most important.

What they bring to each other is balance: The Bull gives the Fish grounding and stability, while the Fish teaches the Bull to dream. Pisces may not understand Taurus's emotional attachment to things, such as a good car, a comfortable home, and solid furniture, but Pisces will feel just as secure with these things as Taurus does.

Other similarities emerge after these two get to know each other. The Bull prefers to stay at home, entertaining a few friends, while Pisces, who enjoys an active social life, also enjoys quiet solitary activities at home.

However, these preferences could turn into a source of conflict for this pair. While the Bull hates to try anything new, Pisces needs new people and new ideas to stimulate its imagination and fend off boredom.

Too much cozy togetherness might also cause Pisces to hit the bar and Taurus to raid the refrigerator. To avoid these temptations, these two will have to diversify their activities. Pisces may have to coax the Bull out of the house—but doing so will keep these two out of a rut.

Taurus is usually patient and placid. But if the Bull is pushed too far, its temper can become uncontrollable and

share their thoughts and feelings honestly. Both the Fish and the Twins play with truth—Pisces because the truth is often too harsh, and Gemini because entertainment is more important than accuracy. This practice can cause confusion and undermine their confidence in each other.

This combination may have little stability, but it has lots of fun. Sexually, Gemini can teach Pisces a few new games, while Pisces' fantasy trips delight the Twins. And if Pisces uses a lighter touch, and Gemini explores a few depths, this couple could share many laughs and delightful adventures.

Pisces with Cancer

(June 22–July 23)

Since Pisces and Cancer are both emotional water signs, they are sure to feel a strong bond from the start. There is a significant difference in their makeup, however. Pisces' emotions are a reaction to those of others; Cancer's emotions can influence the feelings of others. For example, when a friend is sad, Pisces sympathizes, but Cancer lifts the friend's spirits.

Nature protects both of these sensitive signs by giving them a strong instinct for self-preservation. Pisces tends to avoid aggression by swimming away from conflict. Cancer, the mother of the zodiac, is a fierce defender of itself and its loved ones and will meet the enemy head on.

At first, the protective Cancer may seem like the ideal mate for the sensitive Fish, but after a while, the Crab's manner may become more possessive than protective. If it senses a hook, Pisces could obey its instinct to swim away at once.

To Cancer, financial security equals emotional security, so the Fish's more

casual attitude toward money could be a source of conflict. Letting Cancer handle the finances or the business end of this relationship is usually the best solution.

Pisces tends to be more adventurous than the cautious Crab. The Fish enjoys novelty, while Cancer prefers the familiar. The home is the center of Cancer's life, while an active social life and exposure to new people and surroundings are vital for restless Pisces. The Fish feels stifled in the same atmosphere night after night. Not so for Cancer, who is most content in a comfortable, secure nest.

Though this couple are emotionally compatible, they tend to mirror and magnify each other's fluctuating moods.

When both are happy, they are ecstatic. When both are blue, they are desolate.

Sexually, these signs harmonize blissfully, blending Cancer's tenderness with Pisces' imagination. The protective Crab creates a secure atmosphere where the Fish's passion can soar. And the Fish encourages the shy Crab to live out its favorite fantasies.

With their mutual understanding and sensitivity, these two have all the tools they need to work out any differences and enjoy lasting togetherness.

Pisces with Leo

(July 24–August 23)

P isces and Leo complement each other in many ways. For both, the world is a stage where each plays its part happily. Pisces is the character actor, able to change from role to role and to make the other actors look good. And Leo, of course, is the star, always wanting to look good and getting the loudest applause.

There's a strong attraction between

these two. The Fish is drawn to bright, shiny objects, and Leo, the most flamboyant of the fire signs, definitely has flash.

In turn, Leo finds attentive, sensitive Pisces unbearably sexy. Like a cat watching a fish, Leo can become completely absorbed with Pisces and often makes the first move. Yet, if the Lion pounces, the Fish may dart away. A few discreet purrs will get Leo's seductive message across much better.

In this relationship, the kingly Lion becomes a servant, conquered by the seeming helplessness of Pisces. The protective Lion wants to give the Fish the security to explore its world of fan-

tasy and emotion—a world Leo envies. So the Lion gives up its dislike of practical matters and takes over mundane tasks like bill paying and grocery shopping. However, the Fish can be surprisingly clever at finance, finding creative solutions to the many money problems that could develop for this extravagant pair.

Both Pisces and Leo are flirts, but in neither case does a casual batting of eyelashes lead to infidelity: They are simply trying to get more attention.

Sexually, imaginative Pisces is the perfect foil for Leo's sense of drama. This super romantic couple won't be afraid to pull out all the erotic stops. And

both can give the warmth and attention that each one needs.

On the down side, Leo, though generous by nature, can be domineering. The Lion usually pushes its partner to the point of fighting back, then backs off. The problem is that Pisces won't fight, confront, or criticize, so Leo may not get the essential resistance it needs to avoid becoming a bully.

Nevertheless, Leo can be a very good partner for Pisces if the Fish makes an effort to communicate more directly and the Lion learns to tone down its aggressive behavior.

Pisces with Virgo

(August 24–September 23)

Virgo cares about how things work; Pisces cares about how things feel. Can this combination of earth and water signs find common ground?

Virgo's earthly concerns, such as paying bills and keeping appointments, might seem petty to Pisces, and the Fish's dreaminess might seem flaky to the Virgin. Yet deep in their hearts, this

pair would like to have a few of each other's talents. Together, they can enjoy the best of both worlds.

First, though, they must know who they're dealing with, not easy for opposite signs of the zodiac. Virgo understands the world by pulling it apart and examining how everything fits together. This sign will analyze how the couple operates and determine how each can fulfill the emotional needs of the other.

To Virgo this is common sense; to Pisces this is blasphemy. Feelings cannot be analyzed like a flow chart, and cold mechanics cannot be applied to the imagination, which is Pisces territory.

For the Fish, the Virgin is missing the point: Feelings make life worthwhile.

In practice, Pisces might choose a home because the rooms give it a warm, secure feeling. Virgo's choice would be based on such things as square footage and closet space.

In spite of their differences, these flexible signs can easily coexist, especially in a business atmosphere. Virgo analyzes things for the purpose of improving them, and the Virgin's efficiency can help Pisces turn its dreams into reality. Virgo will demand clarity and purpose from the Fish, who tends to get by with vague promises and smooth evasions.

The downside is that, even with the

best intentions, Virgo's critiques could hamper Pisces' creativity. The Fish needs praise and support more than critical analysis.

Sexually, this is a case in which "opposites attract." Lovemaking comes naturally when earthy Virgo passion is unleashed by the sensitive, responsive Pisces.

Both signs may be hesitant to make a commitment, and both need freedom within a relationship. But this compelling union has much to offer if each will accept the other's innate differences.

Pisces with Libra

(September 24–October 23)

S ince neither the swaying Scales nor the darting Fish likes to make the first move, it's usually an outside catalyst that brings Libra and Pisces together. Perhaps the imaginative Pisces and the artistic Libra will meet at work or mutual friends will bring these two together.

This pair has strong potential, but they must forge a unique relationship

that balances their very different emotional needs.

Libra, the sign of the Scales, seeks fairness and balance in all things. Because it sees all sides of any issue, Libra has difficulty making decisions. Romance is one of the few areas where it isn't ambivalent: Libra needs a special partner in life to feel fulfilled.

Pisces, on the other hand, needs emotional involvement with a wide range of people and is not as thrilled to be part of a "couple." To the freedom-loving Fish, Libra can seem too clinging, while the sign of the Scales sways off balance if there is no one on its arm. And when the Fish goes off on a soli-

tary fantasy trip, Libra feels abandoned.

Like other air signs, Libra is ruled by
logic and prefers to have everything
spelled out. Pisces operates by intuition
and inference. So if Pisces suddenly
bursts into tears at the mall, Libra will
look for a logical cause, never guessing
that a little girl walking by reminded
Pisces of a beloved long-lost cousin.

It is easy for this couple to lose focus
and direction. Since Libra has difficulty
making decisions, even ordering dinner
in a restaurant can be a problem. And
Pisces is no help, since this sign reacts to
other people rather than taking the lead.
Common goals and lots of shared inter-

ests are required to hold these signs to-gether.

One common bond is that they are romantics. Libra is the old-fashioned type who responds to hearts and flowers. Pisces is a thoughtful, attentive lover who never forgets birthdays or Valentine's Day.

Sexually, these two intrigue each other. Sensuous, creative Pisces thrills romantic Libra, who responds with artistic flair. If this couple can strike the right balance in other areas, there is much potential for happiness in this relationship.

Pisces with Scorpio

(October 24–November 22)

F rom the moment Pisces feels the penetrating gaze of a smitten Scorpio, the Fish is hooked. But even if the members of this combustible combination can't seem to live without each other, the question remains whether they can live *with* each other.

Though both are highly emotional water signs, they have significant differences. As a fixed sign, Scorpio is far less

adaptable than mutable Pisces. The Fish swims through life with great freedom, knowing it can flow with the tides. Scorpio, on the other hand, goes to great extremes to control every situation in order to protect itself from life's nasty little surprises.

Sometimes their differences can work for this couple, however. While Pisces' emotions are ever changing, Scorpio's are steady, and the sustained power of the Scorpion's passion is intoxicating to Pisces. Sexually, this union is dynamite, with Pisces' fantasies igniting Scorpio's intense desire. Sheer chemistry is enough to keep these two together.

There are some challenges for this

pair. The sociable Pisces must deal with Scorpio's jealousy. What's more, unlike the Fish, who swims away when it gets hurt, the Scorpion will nurse a grudge for years, then get even.

For Scorpio, it won't be easy to counteract Pisces' self-doubts, which are a mystery to the self-assured Scorpion. And the Fish's lack of clear goals might conflict with Scorpio's need for direction in life.

Each sign has traits that can drive the other crazy, especially if they live together. Pisces is comfortable with clutter, while Scorpio needs order to feel in control. Socializing can also become an area of tension. Scorpio prefers a small circle of best buddies. Pisces needs a

range of people and experiences, and conflict is inevitable when the Fish tries to broaden their social horizons.

A strong psychic link keeps these signs in tune with each other, even when separated. When a Pisces business deal closes, Scorpio senses it before the phone rings. This couple's mutual intuition is so strong that keeping secrets from each other is impossible.

When this relationship succeeds, Pisces can teach Scorpio how to face the world with less fear. And the Scorpion can help the Fish learn how to swim through life more decisively.

Pisces with Sagittarius

(November 23–December 21)

isces and Sagittarius share a spirit of adventure. An enthusiastic fire sign, the Archer views the world as a wondrous playground full of potential playmates. Water sign Pisces is constantly exploring a world of dreams and fantasies.

Though excited by each other's questing, restless temperament, and vivid imagination, this combination of mu-

table fire and water signs needs common goals and a clear sense of direction to work. Otherwise, the Archer may gallop off and the Fish dart away after the first fight.

One potential problem is communication. To Sagittarius, life is as simple as the plain truth. The Archer always declares exactly where he or she stands. But for Pisces, nothing is simple: Everything is relative, especially the truth. The Fish is indirect, dropping clues about what it wants and needs.

If the Archer's bluntness becomes excessive, it can wound Pisces. To the sensitive Fish, honesty is fine, but kindness is more important. To handle Pisces, the

fiery Archer must learn to speak in a tactful, nonthreatening way. In turn, the Fish must learn to open up and discuss its feelings.

In addition to communicating, one difficult area for these two is taking on practical responsibilities. Neither will do anything if told "you have to." Where money is concerned, someone has to watch the budget, and though neither sign is about to volunteer, Pisces is usually the more creative money manager. Sagittarius is usually the better provider, but the Archer's generosity and devil-may-care attitude about money could leave Pisces feeling very insecure around bill-paying time.

On the plus side, both signs enjoy the stimulation of a large circle of friends. And neither is possessive, so they'll each have the freedom they crave. What's more, they'll love traveling together and exploring the mysteries of life.

Sexually, neither of these restless signs is very monogamous, and if they lack a firm commitment, both might search for novelty elsewhere. But often they stay warm friends long after the romance has cooled. If they don't take each other too seriously, the Archer and the Fish could have lots of fun while the romance lasts—and leave each other laughing.

Pisces with Capricorn

(December 22–January 20)

Can a practical, ambitious, and money-conscious Capricorn get along with a free-spirited Pisces? Surprise! This pairing usually works beautifully.

In many ways, earthy Capricorn is different from watery Pisces. Determined to rise in the world, the Goat ascends with great self-discipline and persistence, traits foreign to the Fish,

who tends toward self-indulgence. Capricorn's need for status symbols is also alien to Pisces.

In order to more easily climb the ladder of success, Capricorn carefully cultivates a cool businesslike facade, which then becomes difficult to drop. Even socially, the Goat has trouble relaxing and having fun. Yet with Pisces, the Goat can loosen up because the Fish intuitively reads its unspoken feelings without passing judgment.

In turn, Pisces is drawn to Capricorn's stability. It would be easy and reassuring to let Capricorn control the finances and other practical matters in this relationship. But it might be wiser

for the Fish to just absorb a few organizational techniques from the Goat rather than surrender all control.

On a deeper level, Capricorn may not relate to Pisces' world of feelings and fantasies where there are no schedules, strategies, or goals. In fact, some negative traits many Pisces show, such as indecisiveness, procrastination, and disorderliness, could drive Capricorn crazy.

However, it is precisely Pisces' familiarity with feelings that allows Capricorn to express the full depth of its passionate nature. Sexually, Pisces treats Capricorn to a sensual fantasy world where the Goat can forget about business and devote itself to pleasure.

Once committed, Capricorn and Pisces often remain loyal and devoted, through thick and thin, as illustrated by Patricia (Pisces) and Richard (Capricorn) Nixon. Like Pat, the Pisces partner often gives up private life to help the ambitious Capricorn achieve its goals. Though worldly power is not important to the Fish, this sign unconsciously takes on the qualities of the one it loves or associates with.

As this relationship matures, a more relaxed Capricorn and a more stable Pisces will learn to appreciate each other more and more.

Pisces with Aquarius

(January 21–February 19)

Pisces emotion versus Aquarius logic is a key issue that can make or break this couple. Like other air signs, Aquarius is intellectually oriented and would rather not deal with emotions, which can get messy. Logic and reason can be understood; emotion cannot. Those born under the sign of the Water Bearer aspire to be like Mr. Spock.

Logic rarely influences Pisces. Intuition

is a better guide through its world of feelings. When Pisces tries to share its emotions, Aquarius, who wants to be friends first and lovers later, might be standoffish. Or the Water Bearer could analyze Pisces' feelings into nothingness.

Intimacy is a difficult issue for Aquarius, who loves humanity and can expertly handle large groups of people yet is as awkward as a teenager one-on-one. Although full of ideas on how to change the world for the better, Aquarius declares its independence if asked to alter its own life.

Intimacy is sometimes difficult to achieve for Pisces as well. Often those deep feelings the Fish wants to express

have no name, so it tends to communicate with others indirectly.

This pair also has other communication problems. Truth is relative to Pisces, who colors the facts to make them more palatable. To Aquarius, truth is eternal and absolute, and any shading or bending of it is no different than telling a lie.

However, when Aquarius's visionary qualities combine with Pisces' imagination, this can be a very creative relationship—as friends or as business partners. These two signs work very well together in any artistic endeavor, with Aquarius providing the framework and Pisces the inventiveness. Unfortunately, neither

partner is very interested in money, so building up a nest egg or keeping the books balanced could be a stumbling block.

Sexually, Aquarius might be a bit remote for Pisces, who thrives on passion as well as technique. However, this couple can enjoy many pleasant surprises together if they focus on the more inventive side of lovemaking.

Sometimes an unconventional arrangement works best for this odd couple, such as living in separate apartments. By making their own rules and striving to communicate clearly, this relationship could thrive—and last.

Pisces with Pisces
(February 20–March 20)

T hough they may be meeting for the first time, two people born under the same sign can never be strangers. This is especially true for two Pisces. They instinctively understand that they share the same values and motives, even if they behave differently.

To outsiders, two Pisces might look like cold fish, making few public displays of affection. But what no one sees

is the constant telepathic communication and intense emotion they reveal only in private. This couple shares a real intimacy. They don't need to reveal their secrets or tell each other their life stories. Intuitively, they know all they need to know about each other.

The Fish is rarely open because it never wants to say anything that could hurt anyone. But with another Pisces, the Fish can be totally honest, without the risk of hurting or being hurt.

As these sympathetic sign mates get to know each other, they will either reinforce each other's strengths or magnify each other's weaknesses. The danger, of course, is the latter situation. If both

partners are in a "down" mood, they could reinforce this sign's negative qualities, such as self-pity or substance abuse. It is important for them to recognize danger signals and support each other by setting limits and resisting temptations.

In fact, mutual support, rather than romance, is the main benefit of this relationship. Since no other sign has as complex a vision of life, only another Pisces can truly understand a Pisces.

The affairs of the world are not important to these two. Neither cares about attaining wealth or fame. Their shared spirituality and need to care for others propel them through the waters of life. This couple will listen patiently to a

lonely child, feed an abandoned cat, or volunteer in a homeless shelter—all as a matter of course.

Sexually, these two are soul mates who can delight in hours of pleasure. Both are gifted lovers who respect each other's sensitive feelings while exploring each other's fantasies.

By the world's standards of ambition and power, two Pisces are too low key to achieve those things others value so highly. Yet if understanding and love are a high priority, these two signs are an excellent match indeed.

your lover wants to play Scrabble? This could be an Aries-Gemini combination.

To discover more about your relationship, find out your lover's sun sign and look under the appropriate combination. You may learn things you had never even suspected.

Careers and Goals

P isces' success in any career depends on whether the job allows the Fish to exploit its natural sensitivity, imagination, and creativity. Routine or boring jobs or rigidly structured organizations are stagnant waters for the innovative Fish.

The advertising, film, television, and music industries all attract Pisces, although this sign is often more comfort-

Pastimes

L istening te
waves and the
relax. Pisces is a perfect way for
or looking at it refreshes the Pisces soul.
It's not surprising that this sign breeds
avid fishermen, water-skiers, and swimmers. Being in a pool, a river, a lake, or
an ocean—even a bathtub—is like going
home to the Fish.

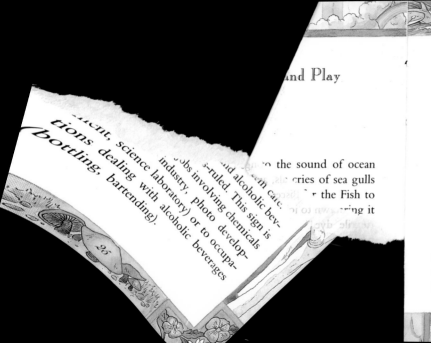

and Play

...ment, science laboratory) or to occupations dealing with alcoholic beverages
(bottling, bartending).

...obs involving chemicals
industry, photo develop-

...o the sound of ocean
...cries of sea gulls
...r the Fish to
...ing it

...and alcoholic bev-
...ruled. This sign is

model of order. But then, if everything were neat as a pin, delightful accidents would never happen, like discovering cousin Lois's photo stuck in a copy of *Anna Karenina*. Pisces would rather be delighted (or sad, for that matter) than neat and tidy.

As a child, Pisces is original and eager to please but dislikes rigidly organized activities, such as scouting. As a parent, Pisces finds discipline a sticky issue because it dislikes imposing rules on others. Instead, it prefers to communicate in the unspoken language of compassion and feeling that children, especially infants and teenagers, understand.

Careers and Goals

P isces' success in any career depends on whether the job allows the Fish to exploit its natural sensitivity, imagination, and creativity. Routine or boring jobs or rigidly structured organizations are stagnant waters for the innovative Fish.

The advertising, film, television, and music industries all attract Pisces, although this sign is often more comfort-

model of order. But then, if everything were neat as a pin, delightful accidents would never happen, like discovering cousin Lois's photo stuck in a copy of *Anna Karenina*. Pisces would rather be delighted (or sad, for that matter) than neat and tidy.

As a child, Pisces is original and eager to please but dislikes rigidly organized activities, such as scouting. As a parent, Pisces finds discipline a sticky issue because it dislikes imposing rules on others. Instead, it prefers to communicate in the unspoken language of compassion and feeling that children, especially infants and teenagers, understand.

able in the background than in the public eye. For example, the Fish may be found behind the scenes working as a creative makeup artist or set designer.

Because Pisces rules hospitals, many enter the medical profession, especially careers that involve patient contact, such as general practice or long-term care.

Drugs, chemicals, and alcoholic beverages are also Pisces-ruled. This sign is often drawn to jobs involving chemicals (textile dye industry, photo development, science laboratory) or to occupations dealing with alcoholic beverages (bottling, bartending).

Pastimes and Play

Listening to the sound of ocean waves and the cries of sea gulls is a perfect way for the Fish to relax. Pisces loves water! Just hearing it or looking at it refreshes the Pisces soul. It's not surprising that this sign breeds avid fishermen, water-skiers, and swimmers. Being in a pool, a river, a lake, or an ocean—even a bathtub—is like going home to the Fish.